IF JESUS WERE GAY

IF JESUS WERE GAY

Emanuel Xavier

A Rebel Satori Imprint
Bar Harbor, Maine

Printed in the U.S.A. by
Rebel Satori Press
P.O. Box 363
Hulls Cove, ME 04644

Copyright © 2010, 2020 by Emanuel Xavier

All rights reserved. Except for brief passages quoted in newspaper, magazine, radio, television, academic articles or online reviews, no part of this book may be reproduced in any form or any means, electronic or mechanical, including photocopying, recording, or information or retrieval system, without the permission in writing from the publisher.

ISBN: 978-1-60864-151-2

Library of Congress Control Number: 2020950759

publication credits

Grateful acknowledgment is made to the following publications in which these poems first originally appeared:

"Outside", "Clean" and "A Simple Poem" appeared in *Bullets & Butterflies: queer spoken word poetry*, 2005 (edited by Emanuel Xavier, suspect thoughts press)

"Abandonment" and "The Untitled Poem" appeared in *Lodestar Quarterly*, 2005.

"The Death of Art" appeared in *Mariposas: A Modern Anthology of Queer Latino Poetry*, 2008 (edited by Emanuel Xavier, Floricanto Press)

"Bastard" and "Just Like Jesus" appeared in *Queer & Catholic*, 2008 (edited by Amie M. Evans and Trebor Healey, Routledge)

"Walking With Angels" appeared in *A&U*, Summer 2008.

"Negative" appeared in *The Gay & Lesbian Review Worldwide*, November-December 2009.

contents

JUST LIKE JESUS	1
PASSAGE	3
FYI	5
ABANDONMENT	7
WAITING FOR GOD	8
WITHOUT RHYME	9
RESOLUTION	11
9	13
ACCESSIBLE	15
ABSTRACT OF A TEARDROP	16
THE MEXICAN	17
REFUGE	18
YEAH	19
NEGATIVE	20
THE PROFESSIONAL BACHELOR	21
REALIZATION	22
EX-BOYFRIEND	23
SOMETHING TO BE SAID FOR SILENCE	25
MORNING AFTER THE COCK	27
FUNERAL FOR A SOUL MATE	29
MUSE	31
RESURRECTION	32
SHOULD I GO DEAF	34
THE UNTITLED POEM	35
SISTER DRUM	37
WALKING WITH ANGELS	39
INVOCATION	41
OF GOD AND NATURE	42
LOVE (for lack of a better title)	44
CARVINGS	45
REGRET	46
LITTLE PRINCE	47
FOR FUTURE POETS	49
URBAN AFFECTION	51
THE UNINTERRUPTED BINDING OF ISAAC	53
SISTA	54
THE "L"	55
WHAT I NEVER TOLD YOU ABOUT PROSTITUTION	56
FATHER	58
SLASHER PICS AND PRIMETIME SOAPS	59
OLD MAID	61

HILLSIDE	63
THE GHOST IN YOU	65
THE NEW YEAR'S KISS	66
PEACE	67
SACRED HEART	68
THE FOURTH KING	69
MIKE FROM ASBURY PARK	71
AWKWARD	72
THE WE JUST WENT OUT ON ONE DATE BUT I REALLY LIKE YOU HAIKU	73
BASTARD	74
SOUND X	75
LIFTING OF THE VEIL	76
THE OMEGA HAS BEEN POSTPONED	78
COMMUNION	79
IF JESUS WERE GAY	80
OUTSIDE	82
CLEAN	84
A SIMPLE POEM	87
THE DEATH OF ART	90
SONGS OF INNOCENCE	92

THIS COLLECTION IS DEDICATED
TO MY MOTHER
WHO TAUGHT ME ABOUT JESUS

SPECIAL THANKS

Sven Davisson, Leo Toro, Shelly Weiss, Rodney Allen Trice, Stephanie Holley, Brandon Lacy Campos (RIP), Gonzalo Casals, Bob Holman, Suheir Hammad, Regina Vogel, Michael Musto, Steven G. Fullwood, Trebor Healey, Cheryl Boyce-Taylor, Tim Miller, El David, Lorant Duzgun,
& all my amazing fans for believing in me

"I like your Christ. I do not like your Christians. Your Christians are so unlike your Christ."
–*Mahatma Gandhi*

"i wanted to write
a poem
that rhymes
but revolution doesn't lend
itself to be-bopping"
—Nikki Giovanni

IF JESUS WERE GAY

JUST LIKE JESUS

Just like Jesus,
I want nativity and childhood
to be simple introductions
Summarized to make way
for the mythology of adulthood
Evading early suffering and teen angst
to grant the world peace
Not only celebrated with mass spending during my supposed birth
but always

I want to encourage and motivate just like Jesus–
An uneducated peasant with spoken word skills
few academic literates could ever conquer
Simply by having faith in what I say
I want to arouse revolution

I want to comfort just like Jesus–
make you believe there is a God above
watching over us
Without need for proof or scientific explanation

Just like Jesus,
I want to cast out your demons and disease
Cleanse your feet with mother's tears; the scented hair of prostitutes
Liberate your oppressed soul from the possession of others
Bring back lost friends from their tombs

Just like Jesus,
I want to create my own family and break with tradition
Host gatherings and feast with sinners and whores
Be a shameless pervert and deviant
while indulging in the subservient role
of feeding the hungry

Instead of miracles,
I want to document my own history
Derail power hungry men from the possibility
of integrating sexism and paternalism
to burden society with guilt and sin

I want to build my own cross with carpenter hands
Carry it down the streets where I will be found bleeding
Pierced with wounds not self-inflicted

Just like Jesus,
I want to hear the voice of my father
Sacrifice myself in his name— arms stretched out
Bask in the brightness of stars with lifeless eyes
Aware this preposterous death is not an end but a beginning
Offering this body to be devoured by scavenger dogs
and birds of prey
a sepia toned symbol of martyrdom

I want my image captured
to snatch the breath out of the oppressor's mouth
Leave them powerless to recreate my looks
to frame the minds of ignorance
launch crusades, sponsor slave ships
and stage brutal wars
while blindly following the utterance of selfish leaders

Just like Jesus,
I want to be nestled half-naked against your chest
Sanctified,
even after my time spent with over a dozen lovers
Claiming your spirit when I come
Baptize you with the promise of salvation

Just like Jesus,
I simply want to live before I die

PASSAGE

Had they known I was gay they would have killed me
None of my poems about peace and unity
would have kept me whole
My thick skin, my loud mouth, my anger, my fists
The God above who watches over everything
Nothing would have prevented death
The redefining of machismo taught by fathers
they never even met

At the age of three, I already experienced
the damage men would do to establish manhood
My spirit had already been destined to be destroyed
at the brutal hands of my own brothers
There have always been men aware of this fate
Lovers willing to risk their lives
and take me with them
Boyfriends who strike when caught in their lies
This blood has tainted many throughout the years
It has not been spilled over foreign wars
or in the name of any flag
It has not been sacrificed for any revolution
or to save someone else

My soul has been sold many times over
during childhood, for a few dollars,
in the name of love
Whoring myself to regularly recapture lost innocence

All of this would have only fueled the passion
of fifteen to twenty young men
Apologies would not be considered
Religion would provide no reason for regret
Mothers would celebrate their sons as saints

Though I was raised on these streets,
there is no right for me to walk them
Someday I will truly get what I deserve
Men like me looking for trouble, converting little boys,
destroying family values,
luring husbands to sin against wives,
This is not the world where we belong
We are not entitled to protection

The next time I find myself alone on this road
I will already be half-deaf so as not to hear the threat
of their coming
I must remember to remain silent
So as not to disturb the neighbors

FYI

I don't really care that you live miles away.
I just need to know that you think of me sometimes,
and that you felt something different
when we first kissed.

I think it's great that we were born only months apart.
I like that you're a geek and I'm a diva but,
like everyone else, we still believe in love,
laughing at ourselves and the joy of life.

I don't really care that all we share on a daily basis
is the moon and the stars.
I just need to know that you have also overcome
great sadness and tears
healed your heart and soul with faith,
moved past the treacherous roads of life's journey
and no longer walk alone lost in a miserable forest.

I just need to know if you could deal
with our past histories
with no judgment or regret over the decadent
and colorful and simply plain stupid.

I just need to know that you could be happy,
celebrate on the dance floor
with sheer abandon and feel the music
without drugs, inhibition, shame,
aware others are staring enviously at fools in love.

I don't really need to know if you have found comfort with others
because of this ill-fated distance between us
I just need to know that you are comfortable
with me in your heart

and that you trust no one could ever take
what we share.
I just need to know that you would protect us
from unnecessary hurt
be honest with yourself and not fall apart
in the face of human nature.

I just need to know that you could feel the sun in spite of the clouds
and that you enjoy the rain even if it causes certain damage
because there is always something beautiful to look forward to.

I just need to know if there is room for disappointment
and you are still willing to walk across the bridge with me
without trying to jump or push me in to the water down below.

I don't really care that there is a time difference
when we speak on the phone,
or that the economy is bad and we're both practically broke.
I just need to know that the weight of the world
will not hold you down
and you will not wait for permission to follow your dreams.

I don't really care to know how many others you have been with
or how many times you have fallen in love.
I just need to know that you will hold my hand
as we are both being stoned for our sins without regret.

I don't really care to know what you may have heard, read, or
fancied about me.
I just need to know that you believe in how I feel about you
when the truths and lies subside.

All I really care to know is that you are aware
of the beauty within you
and that you have somehow changed my life.
I really loved you
and that is all you really need to know.

ABANDONMENT

Somewhere between the restless whispers
and silent promises,
before this war even reached the homeland,
ex-lovers lingered like relapses and fractured friendships staggered
like fresh brush strokes distorting
the unfinished canvas of collaboration

My art has become casualty to a tainted struggle
over land unholy
I have been left blinded by the stillness of abstract portraits of
pleasures past
Intoxicated by the fumes of jealousy

My name will not be lent to this revolution
I will not fall deaf to these bombs
and chorus of laughter
My faith will not die in these battlefields
These bones will not be buried beneath a battle
that is not my own

Terrorists may wander aimless with words as weapons
seeking refuge in the rumors of religions
worth salvation
But as someone who has learned to survive
since the age of three
My advice is to look into the eyes of the enemy

You will soon realize we are all just children
searching to be held by our fathers
hoping they remember our names

WAITING FOR GOD

Officer,
you may choose to disregard this demonstration
Remain as cold as silver badges
As unfeeling as dead sons kissed goodbye by broken mothers

You may choose to claim them unfortunate mistakes
Leaving others responsible
to carry children from cradle to grave
Written off depraved criminals
buried beneath tombs unmarked

Officer,
you may choose to ignore their screams
As you silence the sounds of your fathers
You may choose not to look into their lifeless eyes
Identify them while holding back the fear– your own

Officer,
this is not as simple as racial discrimination
the fingers on the trigger are not always white
Some belong to hands we hold in church during prayer,
recognize from sharing meals at dinner,
remember from being tucked into bed
Defining you the enemy would be difficult
when faces behind guns are often much like ours

Officer,
this poem is not a protest
It is a prayer as we bury our loved ones
Start a revolution to reclaim one ridiculed word
Only celebrated by everyone during holidays
desired before our last breath–
Peace

WITHOUT RHYME

This is the poem I promised
the one that would make you fall in love with me
the one I really write to make you wanna fuck
this is not about you and me
it's about you *in* me
it's about living miles apart
and wanting to be close
if only for one night
maybe just a few

It's about the desire to lay naked with you
make out in the morning
before you have to leave
It's about pretending to be faithful
when we both know monogamy is a lie
the only truth is loneliness
Love is simpler when we dream

This is the poem I write to remember your scent
to taste *el dulce sudor de tu piel*
written with a few Spanish words thrown in
for good measure
to conjure up the heat produced by our tropics
I could've used the word 'pleasure'
but then that would rhyme

It's the one where I try to be all sensual and shit
working myself into a frenzy with my own touch
It's the one about what I'd do with you
If I could control you like this pen

This poem I am writing for you
is with the urgency of not being forgotten

because I enjoyed the dance we shared
the way you held my hand in the theater
How I miss the comfort of your bed
How easy it was to sleep with you

This poem I write is to make you smile wicked
to make you want to tear me apart
expose whatever secrets are left hidden
discover the words, quotes, lines I refuse to write
to leave me broken
with tears of relief

This is the poem I promised
the one that was supposed to make you love me
It turned out to be more about what I had to say
without the sound of my voice
whispering in your ear
because then all you'd hear would be kisses

This is that poem I had to write
Please accept it
It is all I have to give
for now

RESOLUTION

I vaguely recall going to the Roxy.
The uproar of the crowd,
the light display on shirtless bodies
Highlighting hedonism
Dimly aware of the liquor in my system—
the comp admission,
The open bar. My due celebration
Of Gay Pride. Visiting the deejay booth.
I was looking for love, I suppose.
Attempting to capture nostalgia,
Recall youth, with delusional grandeur—
The night and me one decadent darkness,
Like my return to the scene
From the hospital bed, the scars from surgery
Would vanish with morning.

The next day hangover
My lone clear memory.
My brief yet fulfilling dalliance
With being a club kid again.
Painting the town red, for the local fag rags
Of the city to take note. Ignored.
The D-List.
Rules too demanding for me
if only for the time being, nonetheless written down for future reference.
As if nursing a dying Siamese fighting fish
With over feeding
And comparing it to the love of cats
Expecting the same response to a cruel end.

Imagine my surprise when I received a photograph
A close up taken of a large cock

Belonging to one of the guys I apparently made out with
that fateful night
Looming from my cell phone.
Perhaps you wouldn't remember either,
So long ago, about six months,
Haunting me for the holidays. Influencing me
To write a poem.
Never expected
How a simple kiss,
Tongues tortured on the dance floor
This was the symbol
Of my complete recovery,
The cute guy with the hot body and me drunken
Became worthy of literature,
Raw, unapologetic like an erection,
A reminder of temptation
Challenging those winter dates
From the possibility of keeping me warm.

I already knew
After saving the pic as a screensaver,
I was going to remain single.

9

featuring Suheir Hammad

Death comes like wind
sudden and unexpected
It is always wise to count your friends
as you turn a corner
to find out who is left behind buried

wind comes sudden always unexpected your friends a corner left behind buried

In any case, there is always someone missing
drawn to the moon like the sea
claiming their souls to its dry and lifeless wasteland
Some disappear to open arteries or fire
while scars, like passwords, seal our own survival

drawn moon missing sea claiming scars passwords our seal

I live as if by accident
Turning a deaf ear to their screams
Trying to capture their souls before they are gone
fancying myself a poet
praying for paper from the tree of life as words unfurl

unfurl

I walk barefoot along beaches so as to be remembered by the water
Sometimes the sun doesn't shine bright enough
Closing my eyes to reflect the many times
I wished it was my father whose hand curled around mine
as we walked down the planks of the pier

hands curled pier eyes reflect bright enough the sun remembered by water

I never write down the true stories of my life
Sometimes poets just don't care
I leave myself for morning to find
Hoping others will not take up my own death for their purposes

Dedicated to Willi Ninja & Sekou Sundiata

ACCESSIBLE

My most profound moments
are not at a sex club
searching for inspiration
in the eyes of a stranger
as he fulfills the abused child within me
drowned out by house music
and the moans of others

It's lying in my own bed
with my purring cats
on an ordinary night
tranquilito
with a candle lit for St. Therese
soft music playing in the background
the cell phone silent
a pencil slanted in my moisturized hand

ABSTRACT OF A TEARDROP

Please understand when I attended your opening
Before you asked me to meet you secretly
out on the rooftop
I already knew there was art
and somebody else in your life

I will not be the one waiting for you
to come home with the scent of other boys
loving away your needs along the way to maturity
I will not be less than that legend
you make me out to be

The seduction of a poet is splendid indeed
it requires nothing more than a paintbrush, anticipation and a tear

THE MEXICAN

It was rumored you came from far out in Texas
To see my performance in Austin
So when I walked out from backstage
and my Nuyorican eyes rested on your Xicano smile
It brought out the dreamer in me
When a legendary wordsmith introduced us for the first time
It was as if the Virgen de Guadalupe
and all the orishas
Had sanctioned this meeting

... Until I met your *vato*
Estupida,
This poem could have been epic

REFUGE

He hands me a small ring,
probably pewter with black engraved sunshine designs
to remind me of Albuquerque
"I think this will only fit your pinky," he says,
"I got a matching one to wear for myself"

I am only able to afford taking us out to dinner on Indian Row,
cupcakes from Billy's Bakery, and Broadway tickets to see Patti
Lupone in *Gypsy*,
looking forward to the warmth of being
in my hand-me-down bed with him,
and cuddly beasts that wake us up too early
after nights of porn star sex. We would have had so many children,
named them peculiarly. After only six months, we know this is
different

the glow of his smile is my morning sun, mine caught on camera
every time the flash goes off, I wear his scent, trail off with a
whispered 'I love you' every time we're about to hang up, discover
hidden treats for me throughout the apartment, and keep
photographs of him everywhere to keep him close until we're
together again

YEAH

I am silly, come to life with a compliment.
Only submissive in bed, and thick-skinned,
Ferocious like a tiger. An in your face
fuck you to white supremacy.
Caught up in myself like a spider,
Challenging authority as children often do.
Subtle as a dog in heat from my
birthday to that of the one who fulfills prophecy.
Oh St. Therese, my little flower.
Free as wind and intoxicating like alcohol.
Conflicted like the Middle East
An angel without a map, obsessed with porn.
Warm as a Mexican blanket and
comfortable as a beanie bag.
A piranha's mouth, designed for survival.
Funny as a sleeping worm in a box.
Demonized and playful, like a black kitten.
Unapologetic, with scars to show.

NEGATIVE

Because they saved my life, I tell my boyfriend when he asks why I still have a box of condoms on the bottom drawer

next to my bed. There is no real answer. I have never given them much thought as his face becomes suspicious.

That is not the right response, he replies. You are supposed to say you will just get rid of them, searching my eyes

for reassurance. Aware that he has reason to be upset– some were saved from a slot machine in a Buenos Aires

bathroom, some were gifts from foreign men I had met before him– I never realized how much they meant.

I dated a few men who were positive and rubbers were necessary expressions of our love– impressed at any

chance of a relationship for a retired hustler. No matter what I do, everything goes back to that period of my life.

I gave them to my friend the next day.

THE PROFESSIONAL BACHELOR

1. TO THE GUY WITH THE SNAGGLETOOTH IN DC
WHO ASKED ME TO BE HIS BOYFRIEND
WHEN ALL I WANTED WAS A RIDE TO THE BUS TERMINAL

The insanity of my life
does not allow
for the possibility
of a relationship

2. TO THE DIVORCED 5'3" GUY
WITH THE 12-YEAR-OLD DAUGHTER
WHO ASKED ME OUT ON A DATE

That's just way too much baggage
and there's no room in the overhead compartment
(Not that you would be able to reach, anyways)

3. TO THE BAPTIST MINISTER I BRIEFLY DATED

Hey, don't sweat it! At least Jesus loves you!

4. TO THAT GUY FROM PHILADELPHIA
WHO FELL IN LOVE WITH ME AFTER ONLY ONE KISS
AND WISHES HE NEVER MET ME

Why is it that white people can't deal with adversity?

REALIZATION

your voice
is painted in my memory
after so many years
when
you were and always will be rain
and I was earth
you wet
unsettled
and still
your strength makes my ground unstable

this love is older than the sun
it is a church in the middle of the desert
a burning ship out at sea

to love is disruptive
I am not concerned with the chaos
we were both responsible
destroyed our dreams before there was us
you were a kiss from Jesus
my father's presence, a sniff from a cat

you were the dream I always forgot in the morning
I pray your voice never fades

EX-BOYFRIEND

My ex-boyfriend is now HIV positive.
The one who gave me two black cats
I continued to raise as a single parent until
one of them died of diabetes. The one

who came into the bookstore where I worked
to buy a gay travel guide to Florida
because he was moving but decided to stay
with me in New York instead. The one
whom everyone thought was my bodyguard
because he was tall, built, bald and mean looking.

When we first met, we had a lot in
common: recovering addicts,
native Brooklynites, between the
two of us— sex with hundreds
of men. My ex-boyfriend's

family welcomed me as one of their own.
My parents, never comfortable
with my sexuality, actually liked
my ex-boyfriend.

My ex-boyfriend and I moved in together
to an apartment in Jersey City, in an area
surrounded by liquor stores and drug dealers.

He started doing drugs again and
sleeping with other men on the side.
I moved out on my ex-boyfriend and left
him to self-destruct on his own. Instead
of getting the help he needed, he ran off to
do more drugs and have lots of unsafe sex.

He had an older deformed
mentally ill brother, Larry.
"I love you, Manny," Larry would say.
My ex-boyfriend and I played with him,
took pictures with him in silly poses,

put him to sleep at night like our child.
My ex-boyfriend and I discussed
marriage and adoption, we wanted
our own family.

We were the ones who were crazy
looking for salvation in each other,
praying for survival. We did not last for long
and eventually Larry died.

SOMETHING TO BE SAID FOR SILENCE

As a child,
I was often lonely and kept to myself very well
I suppose this explains the reason decades later
I find comfort waking up with strangers
Sharing so much explicitly, perhaps thoughtlessly

I forget sometimes others assume
that they know me completely
Based on what is written in books
or on bathroom walls
Revealing so much of myself
could be the cause for this loss of hearing or work
Or someone I thought could truly be the one

Perhaps, along the way, creating my own family
out of poets and prostitutes
Did not compensate for the lack of ideal brothers
and sisters
Experiences may have seemed the same
but were entirely different
The only thing that may have possibly coincided
was the need to be held

Apparently, you were the only one
to fulfill that same fantasy for all of us
So my name was risked and destroyed
to make this a reality
But what is truth when we deceive ourselves
into believing our own lies
In the end, the greatest revelation could be found
in silence

Others may have tasted these lips

or longed to find themselves that close
but I have bared my soul with only one passionate kiss
meant to be remembered
If you have forgotten or thought it to be simply casual,
Then everything said about me is true
and you were just another poem

MORNING AFTER THE COCK

I awaken hung over again
from one too many Brokeback Mountain Dew's
(Appletini's brilliantly smuggled into the bar
in Mountain Dew bottles)
Look at the guy snoring next to me
I hardly recognize him and I've forgotten his name
I start poking and whispering a soft,
"Hey . . . You . . . Wake Up!'
I look underneath the covers
a mess of lube stains and used condoms
His cock is so Friday night
It's Saturday and I've got things to do
"I have to go home!" I whisper in his ear
I have no clue where I am and this is not the same guy
I remember making out with
My stomach growls and my ass is sore
I ask if he's got cereal or something
He keeps it cute and mumbles,
"The PATH is only a few blocks away"
I am in New Jersey
I AM IN MOTHERFUCKIN' JERSEY!
I am hungry and I don't know what to call him
hence, I give him the stink eye
as he turns to continue sleeping
to reveal an image of the Virgin of Guadalupe
tattooed underneath his hairy back
sporting a mustache and full beard

I get up and gather my belongings
check in the mirror for any signs of hickeys
and dress in the living room
quickly scanning his DVD collection
a copy of *Hannah Montana* slips into my pocket

Outside, the sadistic sun crushes me
mocking the fact, I've been raped again
without breakfast
Maniacally laughing at the comic genius of casual sex
zeroing in on a mind unhinged
por el amor de Dios
Just let me get home safe
and hope there were no video cameras

FUNERAL FOR A SOUL MATE

Sorry to have shot you but I was aiming at my father
Had the bullet not done the job
One of my two black panthers
would've surely mauled you to death
So consider the fact your ultimate end was more pleasant than being eaten alive

I know your worship needed a God
but halos give me headaches
My life was simply too archaic to be religious that way
You see, when I was a child, we lived near a cemetery
and the winds of death still embrace me
like a mischievous prince
Clear balloons in my little hand found
at sacred temples
Where I apparently hungered for any signs
of the messiah
and had an indelible thirst for Jesus juice,
but the world occurred, not much else, not much else

This is surely no excuse
for learning to pull the trigger at the age of three
but you needed to die as my heart was provoked
My Taurean traits were awakened
as my soul recoiled
to the ear-blood stains on my pillow

The moment I sensed any possibility of new love
I descended to my molester's grave
Stared into his dead eyes
to be awakened from this dream
and found this gun in his casket
Now there's nothing left but red

I never wanted to be Christ like
Offering my tears to the only son God ever claimed
to crystallize into powder and snort from a vial–
This may seem sacrilegious to you
but so was the offer to settle down
Living with catastrophe doesn't do much
for self-esteem
and I was not ready for sacrifice
So "ashes to ashes and dust to dust"
and whatever else they say

MUSE

for Willi Ninja

Like a coy diva you haunt discreetly
awakening my thoughts with subtle whispers
prompting me to fulfill the promise
as we held hands from a certain end
the magic already withdrawn from your eyes
forced to walk a destiny arriving too early for the ball

The liveliest memory of us
is parked just outside the piers
under the bright lights of a clear night
Praying to the waters of Yemaya y Oshún

There was no need to ask that I write this poem
Without words or tears, it is lifeless
This is only a shadow of legendary
because it comes from a withered heart
These limbs are already fractured
unable to unlock limitations and click inspiration

Your House is waiting
Your children
stretched across a cold floor
in every pose you left behind
staring at a ceiling without stars
while your mother holds their sorrow

They will dance only to the echoes of your soul
as you dare to claim the clouds under your heels
Myself, I will rest upon the ashes of your dreams
until the sky falls

RESURRECTION

I came back for you
after shaving off all of my hair to reassure your loss
to symbolically unite us as mother and child
flowers to acknowledge the rare celebration
of your magnificence

Picking up a different person
from the one dropped off at the hospital earlier
your eyes haunted me with the memories of drugs
wasted on my youth
almost feeling the poison rush through me

Before putting me out on the streets
I wonder if you had wished you could've kissed
the boy I once was
the childhood spent growing up together
side by side
at the edge of the bed praying for a better life
Nobody ever gave us instructions
on how to be a teenage mother and child

The doctors said it could come to this
I simply wish I could've kissed
the woman you once were
with a more meaningful 'goodbye'
before running away as always
I'd take us back to the day I returned home
and fell into your arms

You are different now but still recognize my voice
laughing away my fear of losing you
I can't imagine what you're going through
but I know what it is to feel alone

and that we both share a survivor's heart
I kneel at the edge of your bed as you lay in pain
con las manos juntas like you taught me
and once again, I pray to forget the past
to forgive and never look behind

Only because of you have I managed
to defiantly survive
Like Jesus, I wish I could look up at the sky
cry out to an unknown father and die for your sins
If God would send His angels
They would find us on the merry-go-round
at Astroland in Coney Island
If I had the right to miracles,
others would have to wait
because this ride simply didn't start on time
and it's never too late to feel the innocence
we never had

When our time comes, it will simply come
Nothing we could do about it
Until then, I will love you
for whom you are today
and who we were yesterday

SHOULD I GO DEAF

If I am incapable of listening to a poem
delivered on a mic
I have faith I will still feel the words
emerge from a page
My hearing is quickly fading
Soon there will be the death of silence
There is so much I never heard
things I never caught myself saying
I've accepted this loss as a higher will
grieved the passing of my pride
I thank all those voices that have inspired me
and pray God sanctify my sight

THE UNTITLED POEM

Nothing is too difficult to consider for poetry
too hard to share with an audience hungry
for revelation
The colors of memories are never too bright
for white pages

The first time he touched me
leaving a lifetime of anger
the many beds I slept on
coffins to rest in peacefully
from the torture of my conscience
before getting up to shower off the blood

Unable to recreate the destruction left behind
the pain I felt as he entered
times I prayed for someone to stop him
how it feels when friends tell me to get over it
or why I've had trouble settling down

This is the darkness I become
when I remember all those I never welcomed
Convinced few could ever understand
But sometimes men are able to find the little boy
huddled on a rooftop staring at the stars
Some men are able to forgive
the small child that picks up a toy
and walks out of the store without paying
Men unafraid to fill the vacant spaces
of an unknown father
Some things are not universal
prostitution and drug use
the brutal moments of children
watching mothers beaten

nights spent on the streets praying for silence
mornings lost wondering when life would begin
bright beautiful days when the breeze
caresses an abused body
and sincere smiles aware of survival

De La Vega says, "Become Your Dream"
So I write to silence nightmares
hoping just one person knows who I am
and who I was
When I whisper my last goodbyes
on the final line of an untitled poem

SISTER DRUM

Dedicated to Stephanie Holley

There are things you should know
This nightmare, splendidly hidden behind a smile,
has haunted me for years
Life was simpler when our innocence was lost
on the dance floor
Naive to the risks involved in trying to touch the stars

The only friend I was never selfish to was a mirror
and the emptiness it reflected
Caught up in my necessary fame
I have been foolish never to appreciate your strength
Capable of tearing down and building graffitied walls

Throughout the years,
you encouraged me to define myself
Welcomed this bard as your brother
and watched him develop consciousness
Listened without prejudice
to revelations about darkness
Men who entered without words
and left a broken child within

I never thought I'd finally write this poem for you
Naturally assuming we would look back
from our rocking chairs someday
Reminiscing about lovers past
(If I could even remember their names)
It is only now I come to realize
you were just as fragile too

I forgot to properly thank you

for taking care of my children while I was away
Busy calling in misguided adventures
of momentary pleasure
Offering only drops of my soul
to satisfy your sacred maternal thirst

I promise to carry you to your place of rest
I will always remember
how your rhythms helped craft my words
Providing the ability of listening to angels
even through deaf ears
On this journey, the sound of your drum
has kept me on the right path home
You should know
your beat has kept me whole

WALKING WITH ANGELS

for Lindsay

AIDS
knows the condom wrapped penetration
of strangers and lovers, deep inside
only a tear away from risk

knows bare minimum t-cell level counts,
replacing intoxicating cocktails
with jagged little pills

knows how to avoid a cure thanks to war
how to keep pharmaceutical corporations
and doctors in business

AIDS
knows the weight loss desired by supermodels,
knows the fearless meaning
of a friends genuine kiss or hug
converts non-believers to religion and spirituality

comprehends loneliness
values the support of luminaries
smiles at the solidarity of single red ribbons

knows to dim the lights to elude detection
how to shame someone into hiding
from the rest of the world
to be grateful for the gift of clothing and shelter,
to remain silent,
holding back the anger and frustration

AIDS

knows that time on earth is limited for all of us
that using lemons to make lemonade is better than drinking the
Kool-Aid
but no matter how much you drink
you are always left dehydrated

knows working extensive hours
to pay hospital bills, the choice of survival
or taking pleasure in what is left of life

knows the solid white walls
you want to crash through and tear down
the thoughts of suicide in the back of your head

AIDS
knows the prosperous could be doing more
with their wealth
and that everyone still thinks it is a deserving fate—
for gays, drug addicts, prostitutes,
and the unfortunate children of such
born into a merciless world
of posh handbags and designer jewelry

knows how to be used as another percentage
to profit politicians
knows it doesn't only affect humans but animals too, without bias
—providing fodder for art
and something to be left behind

if there is a God
he has disregarded our prayers
left his angels behind to journey along with us
—none of us knowing exactly where we are headed

INVOCATION

for Dominic Brando

It is said the gift of art
is our hearts expressed are
free and the rhythm
releases
our souls
I listen to your songs
remind myself of your laughter
intoxicating; full of life
inspiring these words for you
offer this prayer
to tattoo on your back grant
you peace with this
poem
hope you possibly find the truth
about love
at last know why we exist
to learn
why we dream
to escape
These words I hope you hear
remember your smile
was god and the heavens
realize your spirit
is finally free

OF GOD AND NATURE

This is for that gorgeous, sexy *papi chulo*
teaching brown-skinned schoolchildren
'bout *Americano* dreams
seemingly dangerous, full of passion,
with shaved head and wicked smile

Driving his radiant pickup truck
under the San Antonio sun,
enjoying an afternoon beer at the local bar,
looking out for his homeboys,
Praying to ancient, forgotten deities,
feeding stray one-eyed cats,
sitting on back steps and staring at the moon,
Shirtless, enjoying the breeze, remembering our kiss,
wearing nothing else
than second-hand basketball shorts,
Chinese *chanclas,* rosary beads, *escapularios,* multiple tattoos
and a hard-on stiffly pointing up
towards the star-filled sky

I don't know what you've done
to make me hunger for your taste
this longing to bare my soul to you
more than to any other man
What could I possibly expose to you
I haven't already to the world
Will writing these words keep all of this real
justify and bless this radical affair
This poem will not clarify the need to hold your unguarded self
in my arms,
inhale your scent, mourn your dead,
unfold your mysteries,
Would it be wrong to admit I'd give up everything

If in your eyes, I saw you felt the same

Close or faraway, I still feel your lips taking my back
aware this craving is not just about
entertaining the possibility of sex with you
(I truly enjoyed sex with you)
It is about finding the place in ourselves
where nothing else matters
When we could look out into the rivers
from which we came
and simply say, "It's beautiful out here"
knowingly expressing this passion
Revealing secrets to each other and our gods
and no one else
Wouldn't you already know how much
you mean to me
Would I have to place my hand on your chest
silently pass these feelings on to you
with a tender touch
so that you could sense *mi corazón*
You would never have to engrave my name
across your ribs
because I will already belong to you completely
No words, phrases, epic poetry could ever capture
the *mariposa* that is the beauty of our love
It is winged, it is free, and it is nature

LOVE *(for lack of a better title)*

It's just another man
holding me close
as we stare out into the Hudson River

Of course, we'd be at the West Side Highway piers
with the moon light shining over New York City

There would most certainly be a soothing,
gentle breeze
We wouldn't have to say a single word
No one would bother us

It would just be two guys
a song in our heads
a smile on our faces
and the memory of all who came before

CARVINGS

We are the same, hopeless romantics,
this time with reason:
me, a survivor, therefore each day is special:
when you say, "I love you," I remember
a bird's song, a children's Saturday morning
television program with a puppet squirrel,
a Van Gogh painting and drawing
comic book characters underneath a Brooklyn tree:
tu eres an inspiration of photographs, sound,
and laughter, branches spread throughout memory
as if you were an oak, your scent is
always autumn, the breeze– calm and refreshing
(tall against the sky, night winds caress your leaves),
protecting me outside the window:
bearing fruit in the spring, climbing your shoulders to see the
universe, the gentle rain
providing life, in mine where there
have only been storms, you shelter me,
raising me above the floods
with new breath, baptizing this union with
your lips, your kisses are my salvation, sanctifying (thunder and
lightning have disappeared, rainbows instead): this heart is rooted,
because you,
a sort of refuge and comfort, a poem in the end,
are a haven with which to enjoy the world

REGRET

Thanks to you, I regret staying away from the comfort of our bed and limit my travels to just a few days.
    I long for your caress
I try to remember the smell of your hair
What is the sound of your sweet kiss against my ear?
Thanks to you, I love lying around cuddled with nothing to do and no care in the world, even though so much is going on outside our window.
    I want to remember the sound of you awakening me in the morning
I want to remember your soft touch.
    Like water touching my bare feet and pulling away back into the ocean,
I am left wanting to feel you once again. I am filled with joy when I see one of your kind; if you were to leave, I would go absolutely mad.
    Your tongue soothes me,
like honey on a sore throat.
    I live to feed your hunger,
despite the fact, I often cannot provide for mine.
Thanks to you, there is no one else in the world for me; thanks to you, I avoid the obstacles that would challenge our love: allergic reactions, disdain for animals.

LITTLE PRINCE

Kitty baby, feel me caress your little head
on a sunny day with cool breezes
Close your eyes as I massage
that perfect spot just above them
Lick my fingers with your delicious tuna breath

There goes your brother again, silly
Resting his paw on this page
as I write a poem for you
Rubbing his wet nose against this pen

You are both my childhood dream
Escaping on adventures together
filled with rivers of ice cream
and plenty of trees to climb
Watching animals parade in harmony

Before you catwalk that rainbow to the other side
I want to wish you treats and plush toys
All the affection and comfort you have given me
Fairies that brush you regularly
Fishes in streams of spring water
Mexican blankets that keep you warm
Milk from friendly cows

My baby Sable, always remember my laughter
Never forget me
entertaining one of my two biggest fans
Singing and dancing show tunes and pop songs
for my muses
Rising your ears to sweet kisses and mouthfuls of fur

I'm not much for religion

but if there is a heaven for me
I pray it includes my little buddies
You have taught me love
and that angels come in many guises

FOR FUTURE POETS

To be a poet you must be hopeful and romantic
without understanding why
It is vital to continue dreaming
even when life has taught us no matter
whom we pray to
or which star we choose
none of our wishes will ever come true

It will always be natural to write about suffering
especially when colored
and our friends and loved ones are slowly dying
It will never be easy to share about laughter,
moments of self-realization and inspiration,
the songs we want to sing aloud

Sometimes poets make for lousy friends
always caught up in ourselves
looking for the next compliment
or potential poem or "piece"
listening to each other only to figure out
where we fit in

The passions of poets shift suddenly and unexpectedly
which makes for challenging love affairs
Only our pets are worthy of complete
and undivided attention

We may not be qualified to rule the world
only allowing access to the public side of ourselves
Still, we are not threatening or malicious
For we are simply story tellers
and sometimes we all need something to believe in

Poets gather to the sounds of the oppressed
never wanting to be admired for foolish endeavors
The sheer magnificence of being a poet
is the acceptance of not being free
the way others assume we are
With nothing left to fear, maybe sadness
we continue to smile even when there is war
And there will always be war

Life is a journey we all walk alone
without someone to carry our baggage
we must carry our own notepads and pencils
Learn to enjoy the sound of our own laughter
without a drink in hand
because there isn't more than this

All we have is setting years to look forward to
and scattered friends littering our path
asking to be written about and remembered

URBAN AFFECTION

for Walt Whitman

Besides the obvious technological and architectural advances, only one thing has really changed between our generations:

We now live in an America where blacks are not only allowed the right to vote but can become the Redeemer President of the United States

Otherwise, we still live in an America where the audacity to openly enjoy the pleasures of sex and being respected for wisdom are contradictions without reconciliation

We still live in an America where the economy collapses while the masses are consumed with preventing the rights of anyone with a fancy for anything out of the ordinary

We still live in an America where rotting leaves, tufts of straw, and debris are found in more homes than poetry books

We still live in an America where Christ and Dracula provide both excitement and fear for restless lives longing for a simple touch

We still live in an America where the impact of urbanization reaches out to the common person more than the obscene nature of poetry

We still live in an America where writing about prostitution is considered trashy and profane

We still live in an America where poets have to work while publishing to survive financial difficulty unless they are fashioned like Shakespeare

We still live in an America where, unless you belong to a church, you are a religious skeptic believing in nothing

We still live in an America where overt sexuality, siding with the barnburners, and authoring disreputable books limit poets to a vagabond lifestyle

We still live in an America where breaking tradition and the boundaries of poetic form are considered the trademarks of a pretentious ass

We still live in an America where everything from thieves to dwarfs to fog to beetles deserve validity

We still live in an America where books cannot prevent war and the sick and wounded need healing

We still live in an America where not everyone can appreciate the beauty of immigration, crowded streets, brutal differences, urban affection

We still live in an America where the same sun that once invigorated your passion continues to provide us with the beauty of life worth fighting for

We still live in an America where America still lives in us

THE UNINTERRUPTED BINDING OF ISAAC

for my father
all that I ever was—
an erection, a series of thrusts, an ejaculation,
a random triki traka

When my best friend's father passed away
I didn't know how to feel or what to say
as I never had the love of a father to miss

You never beat me with a ta te quieto stick
You never put food on the family table
You never taught me how to defend myself from bullies
You never protected me from monsters
You never recognized yourself in me

for you I might as well have been a dead child
never mind a street grown poet angry with God
left behind for my love to bleed on concrete
an artist cursed at birth looking for some recognition

every time I see an exposed breast with a tiny infant nursing
I remember my mother and how she was always
cumpliendo la condena
My regrets for being the fastest swimmer
Nonetheless, thank you for teaching me that
humanity is not a right but a privilege

SISTA

I have learned to conceal pain
behind easy, flirtatious smiles
after losing you
somewhere in the decadence
I longed so much to share
Unaware some things are best kept to ourselves

I'd forgotten we're not blood
not carved alike
Creating our own landscapes
Only having endured the same torture as children
to feel at peace with our independence

After all, we're not really sisters by blood
You have your own collection of Barbie's
and photographs
I have my own flashbacks and moments of rage
I have never seen my father's grave
the umbilical cord–
soon it will be buried too

Sometimes the only way to survival
is walking the cemetery alone
If you bother looking for me
inspect the crumbled leaves
you may find a teardrop
it will still be fresh
you will be like family

THE "L"

Sitting on the L train with a friend
I was made aware my voice was getting louder
By one of the men next to us
who came up to ask if I could keep it down

He didn't know about the hearing loss in one ear
So I remained silent without words to explain the hurt
I didn't turn around to expose the scar
on the back of my head
the one I unsuccessfully tried to conceal
by letting my hair grow out
so that I wouldn't have to explain its origin
on dates or job interviews

Instead of business cards,
I should walk around with pre-printed notes
attached to pens
explaining my history and current disability
to distribute on the subway

They would read as follows:

My name is Emanuel and I am a spoken word artist. I am a victim of sexual abuse. I was thrown out at sixteen for being gay. I became a prostitute and a drug dealer. I found my salvation in writing. I published a few books you never heard of and ended up on television on shows you never watched. I was recently attacked on the streets where I grew up. I was then diagnosed with acoustic neuroma. The surgery left me deaf in my right ear and unemployed. I do not do drugs. I am not homeless. I do not have AIDS. Men like me are not allowed to be soldiers yet I am a veteran of war. I am not asking for your money. Please get home safe and keep this pen to share your story too. Maybe someday I will get to hear your voice.

WHAT I NEVER TOLD YOU ABOUT PROSTITUTION

That my mentor was Jay, an HIV positive hustler,
known for his big, uncut Puerto Rican dick
featured with a sense of humor in his tight Speedo's
who looked out for me and loved me like a kid brother

That I used to be picked up regularly by a pedophile
who would drive me around in his car
sharing stories about how he fucked his daughters
Never asking me to do anything
just listen while he parked and jerked off

That I would sometimes sleep underneath these cars
at the West Side Highway piers when it rained
using a tee shirt I bought with my first hustler money
with an image of Dorothy in New York City saying,
"Toto, I don't think we're in Kansas anymore!"
as a bundled up pillow to rest my head and dream on

That a married, closeted man with children
turned to cry and wouldn't let me touch him
as he stood with his back to me in his underwear
making me feel disgusting about myself

That a trick once peed in my mouth
and made me swallow
before making me lick his boots
and held me tenderly in his arms all night

That an older man with a huge cock
(then again, I was sixteen so they were all older)
fucked me bareback in a tiny booth at a bookstore–
left me sore and bleeding with hemorrhoids
unable to get it up the ass and hustle for weeks

That I once picked up a trick
who thought he was a vampire
bit my cheeks, tore into the skin until they bled
and sent me back to the piers– bruised and swollen
forced to wear bandages with no health insurance
went back to visit my mother on Mother's Day
told her I had been jumped and broke her heart

That once, in '88, a stoned black man
stood staring at me early one morning for hours
never approaching me with the sorrow in his eyes
Days later, his picture all over newspaper covers–
he had been Jean Michel-Basquiat, a famous artist
who speed balled to death

That sometimes I actually fell for these men
imagined them being my savior
with nothing more than a comfortable bed to sleep in,
a good breakfast in the morning, a grateful smile
and a few dead Presidents in my pocket

That these were my fucked up formative years
and these men stood in for my father figures
I propose a toast to every single one of them
because none of us ever imagined
that I would be writing about them someday
full of love, life and laughter

FATHER

i spent much of my life
sad never to know you
but how miserable
to have discarded children
to not feel their
cold bodies crying
to sleep.
        i think about time wasted searching
for your eyes   longing
love   lost imprints
as you reproduce with
others unknown in
your drunken stupor,
i imagine your
heart   i long to
crawl into that cave
hieroglyph your walls.
understand
        what you create
thrives on your self
destruction, i pray
with your dreams bloodied on my hands.

SLASHER PICS AND PRIMETIME SOAPS

Your mom would refer to me as *Il Ragazzo Spagnole*. Wonder silently what you had in common with me as we watched Culture Club videos in your living room. We would invite Marco over to play 'Killer' in your basement because we enjoyed being his victims. You were the smartest kid in junior high school and we were all geeks and unaware of it.

One summer, I became a gay hustler, lost whatever innocence I had accrued since I was three. You never would have noticed. Awed by your intelligence, I kept it covert and stuck to you for salvation. Repressed, delusional. Pretending to be anything but myself to avoid the obvious. Grover Cleveland High School tried to contain us. We acted out scenes from 'Dynasty' and cast our friends as characters

in some outrageous primetime soap. There was always a cliffhanger at the end of the semester and we would have to wait to find out who lived and who died. You had an older brother I would always hope to catch shirtless in his bedroom. He had more hair on his chest than our faces and yet we always had our beards. We fancied them our girlfriends. We never kissed, only spoke about boys, and had no sexual interest in each other. They made us feel like

one of the girls and their parents knew they were safe around us. To fit in, I learned Italian because I was the only Spanish one in the group and seldom embraced my own culture. The first time I told you I was gay was appropriately in a college library. I never imagined someday I would become a writer, and less, that you would be shocked. You were not ready to come out yet, scared,

uneasy. The look on your face worthy of a season finale. I withheld from saying anything about that summer, my demise to drugs, and getting involved with someone positive. We were instantly distant, heading down different paths, held together only by memories. Years later, we share stories about our boyfriends around swimming pools in Fire Island. I smile genuinely at our progress. Us, who together attended our first Madonna concert, secretly knew of our first crushes, hid in closets for survival from killers.

OLD MAID

My cats are peaceful,
lying asleep at the edge of the bed
Warm air from a heater comforts them,
this bed, these feet
Ruben calls from the first floor
to make plans for the weekend
After five years living above him,
I have finally become a confidant

Maybe because I am tired of remaining exclusive
to fair weather friends
which no longer require being ushered
past velvet ropes
This name and address mean nothing
once love comes to town
All that is left are lamps, books, and pillows

My sister of sin has run off to the altar
and I find myself a virgin again—
pure and simple
This loneliness is astounding and maddening,
if not necessary
nobody really knows me besides these walls—
olive green and in dire need of a new paint job

These creatures, which share my space
must find me ridiculous
though it is clear, they love me
Before they inhabited my world, it was truly empty
But then I was hardly ever home
Now I cannot wait to open the door
and give them all the attention I need in return
because I realize I also have something to love

These are my reasons to support gay marriage–
better neighbors and good pet owners

HILLSIDE

for Leo Toro & Rodney Allen Trice

The fabulous thing about us
was not that we connected
through sex and alcohol,
sharing nefarious adventures
around a campfire.
Neither was it because we were dubbed
"The Joy Boys"
by all the naked men in the forest,
able to claim they had slept with at least one of us
never remembering our names.
And we never scored anything
more than a mere blowjob
worth a serious relationship,
even though Love is what we really wanted
and there was always the risk of discovering
a new STD.
We traveled many miles together
listening to an iPod, the car crammed
with tents, equipment, condoms, lube and liquor
with crass purpose.
We discussed politics and art.
We laughed at ourselves
inside the teeny blue beetle car
with faux daisies on the dashboard.

Yet, in all our wicked divinity, we failed to realize
that we left some piece of our legend
hidden somewhere on the road to Hillside,
behind the back area of "Wreck" Hall,
along with our Candy Cockrings
and Debutant Ball drag outfits.

Oh Lord, we truly apologize for this belligerent haiku:

Strong winds July Fourth weekend
Tents are not spiked down
Mother Nature, you're a cunt!

Please forgive our sins and watermelon martini's.
Don't forget it was always cold at night
up on those mountains,
sometimes it rained, and still
we always managed to find someone to keep us warm.
Consider we were only trying to convince ourselves
we could live forever in these moments.

THE GHOST IN YOU

It is unfortunate I could never take the place
of your ex
His grave reflecting in your ghostly eyes
Making offerings of pink roses and nine
Echoes of his soul heard through thunder gods
I always imagined us Manhattan towers
defiant against the sky
Yet even those are vulnerable to crumble and get lost
in clouds of ash
What happened in the past
simply happened in the past
Nonetheless, besides gravitational pull,
this love is what keeps me grounded
A tent pitched on a campsite waiting to be saved
by the sun
Though we are bound by revolution
I am allowed only to marry your shadows
Forbidden the sweet taste of your universe
While his essence hangs in moonlight
There will be no subway rides for us
or snowflakes in your hair
As you wait to join forces with the hero of your fears
Words come to me when you do not
Like my father's blank face along the side of the crib
Nothing left to do now but fold these black wings
Continue living in this death
Haunted by the things we didn't get to do
and dreams doomed to appear elsewhere

THE NEW YEAR'S KISS

When we finally made out on the dark dance floor
Of that empty disco, after posing for paparazzi
Prior to years end, after your deejay set, at another club,
Sweet, intoxicated, wet New York City dream
Watched by jealous strangers, and when
You touched me underneath my shirt
As my heart raced with fulfillment, the possible death
Of silence, promiscuity and selfishness
And we left to ride a cab just a few blocks
down to that straight party
To visit the other side of life
The minute we entered
That pivotal time before exchanging text messages
In another calendar, secretly considering a challenging relationship,
I should have realized I was already hauling your baggage
At my own will without much thought
Or regret. Looking back
With sobered eyes I see
Myself ready to give it all up for your Paradise,
My scarred head resting on your chest
A few poems below my belt
Stashed into pockets, and black, furry creatures
Asleep at our feet, guarding us with protective claws,
I failed to acknowledge, so did you
As we parted ways on separate cars
Toward Washington Heights and Bushwick,
That this fabled kiss, fresh with hope,
Joining us both so intimately,
The moment so decidedly more fateful
Bigger than either of us on that passionate night
Was the only sacred thing we could ever share–
sealing our destiny
And unable to predict the future

PEACE

Dear dad,

I'm not angry with you anymore. I don't even know you to say that I hate you. I just wanted you to know that I am doing just fine. Maybe it's simply more important for me to think that you care but I live in Brooklyn with a handsome cat. I had two but one of them died of diabetes. I've had a rough life and written a lot of bad stuff about you, mostly because I needed to get it out of my system. When I was younger, I used to wonder what you looked like. It was kind of fun imagining you were more than just some random guy on the street. In my mind, you had special powers and watched over me. I've done many bad things I suppose thinking maybe I might get your attention. I'm over all of that now. I don't know what kind of life you have but I hope you're sincerely happy. I don't know why you left my mom or me. I know she could be a real bitch sometimes and you probably weren't ready to have me as a child. You might never read this and I might never get to meet you but I just wanted you to know I've survived and made something of myself in spite of it all. I've finally learned how to feel alive. I have found true love and happiness and pray you have too.

Your son,
Emanuel

SACRED HEART

We haven't quite met yet
but you're the only thing that seems promising
in my world currently filled with Parkinson's disease,
cancer remission, unemployment, lost love
I've been crawling my way back home from the Albuquerque deserts
the New Mexican sun left behind for the cold chill of subway stares
the high road to Taos faded from memory
along with the prairie dogs and ice caves
returning to battle wearing the same warrior clothes
hoping to find a glimmer of hope in your eyes
a touch of wisdom in your kiss
a new beginning in your arms
flowers grow on mountains and between cracks in the concrete
You will be sex personified
thick and built solid as a bold text letter
The sky, the air, the wind will be different with you
I will be comforted by your rain
You will write me back to life
Someday we will finally rest

THE FOURTH KING

Sweet baby boy, Christ child,
do not fear me
My eyes may not be the same
supposedly heavenly blue of your Bethlehem gaze
but I come to pay my respects from a future
yet to come.
(For the record, this is why history will forget me
and label me a sorcerer.)
I bring you blood diamonds from Africa;
this fashionable tee shirt
with an image of a revolutionary
who will rise to power to condemn sodomites
in Cuban concentration camps;
and condoms to protect yourself from intimacy
which could lead to disease.
(Never mind . . . I'll just keep these
since they will be useless to a poor carpenter
who believes in abstinence.)

Sweet baby boy, Christ child,
please accept the rest of these offerings
as symbolic and useful to a baby as gold,
frankincense and myrrh.
(I wouldn't be insulted if your parents sell these also
to finance a trip to Egypt.)
These gift items will inspire the world to celebrate
your miraculous birth
with shopping sprees and songs of joy
to drown out the famine, poverty, and suicide rates
and the sounds of children playing
with real machine guns.
There will always be war upon these lands and waters you will learn
to walk upon.

The intoxication of your blood and other cocktails
will help mankind
forget the loss of loved ones and all suffering
on your birthday
until the day you return to fulfill your prophecy.
I pray your angels watch over you
and guard you from pestilent drugs,
which will plague generations to come
with the desire of feeling closer to you.

Sweet baby boy, Christ child,
bless me with your laughter.
(And if any of the other magi touches you inappropriately,
cry until they are deafened by their sins.)
Know that I adore you regardless
of how you may have truly been conceived
and that this day will bring families and friends together.
I hope I get to see you again someday
as I will have many questions for you,
sweet little Emanuel.
I will keep an eye out
for any other astrological signs of your second coming
like natural disasters, global warming
and whatever pamphlets might be handed to me
along my travels.
Until then, in memory of this day,
I will pretend there is peace on earth always
and look forward to another year.

MIKE FROM ASBURY PARK

While sucking him off
I'm wondering about his medical history
and if he will even remember my name
All he knows about me
is how to mix my favorite drink
And that downstairs at the bar
my best friend is waiting
to tell our other friends how I took the bartender upstairs
to our hotel room
And he knows I am a poet from Brooklyn
staying overnight after a gay wedding reception
And I only know he has an amazing chest
and a delicious Italian cock
And when he thrusts forward
he fills the back of my throat completely
And that he has the body of a tattooed God
And that he will cum in my mouth
And I will let him

AWKWARD

One of my cats likes to lick himself on his furry arm
whenever he is happy
It is now discolored
Sometimes he falls asleep with his tongue in motion
This is because it reminds him of his mother
weaning him
She was killed by a car
before she finished nursing the litter

I enjoy sex with insignificant strange men
whenever I am lonely
I've had many lovers
Sometimes I fall asleep in their arms with great ease
This is because I am searching for my father
He disappeared when my mother refused
to have an abortion

Once, my cat lay at the edge of the bed licking himself
as he watched me going at it with some daddy
I felt funny about this so I asked
whatever his name was to stop
In the morning,
after we exchanged awkward goodbyes
I realized I should take a lesson from my cat
and simply learn to pleasure myself

**THE WE JUST WENT OUT ON ONE DATE
BUT I REALLY LIKE YOU HAIKU**

Sunlight bursts through clouds
Sky is no longer broken
Your smile is heaven

BREAKDOWN:

You are so damn hot
Definitely worth my time
It feels like *fuck yeah*

BASTARD

Heard you got knocked up
and I know you don't love him
Please, don't get wed for appearances
This is why I get pissed gays can't marry

Don't listen to family bullshit
Especially my mom's religious hypocrisy
(She didn't even know my pop's last name)

Remember Mary was also an unwed mother
Joseph wasn't even the baby daddy
She only claimed to be a virgin
not to be labeled the whore she was

Shit, back then, if I were Jesus,
I would've claimed God to be my father too

SOUND X

for Lorant Duzgun

it is heard
only when the spirit is silenced
sacred sounds are
heaven and you hear
peace like never before
listen beyond the music
shut out the noise
grab the rhythm
this song for you
follow its soul
bless the beauty
with your ears sense
the cadence of these
words
can you dance
freely and with freedom
enjoy the lights
for splendor the darkness
for clarity
with this heaven always
remember what you hear
is peace
a sound you've never heard before

LIFTING OF THE VEIL

On the operating room table
I dreamt God came down from up above
I was now at Her side
cloaked in secrets
looking back at everyone that thought they knew me

We floated high above Ecuador,
named after the equator, center of the Earth,
We floated high above Puerto Rico,
scanning for any signs of a father
I never met
knowing neither of us would recognize Him
even if we saw Him
We floated high above New York,
past the Christopher Street piers towards Bushwick,
the place where I was raised, called home
and eventually beaten
surrounded by a gang of fallen angels
who never recognized me as their own

God raised Her majestic long black arms
and I remembered as a child
I always knew my life would change at 33
Though this wasn't the sudden death I had imagined
or the Christ Like martyrdom
It was simply the development of a tumor in my head
Unnoticed until I could no longer hear
the spoken word, which had become salvation

God was angry people thought
this was Her punishment
there was war, famine, natural disaster, devastation
God does not gamble

Eventually, I would awaken from anesthesia
silenced forever only in one ear
and learn to smile again
though most would forget
I was almost left half a motionless face

It was heaven to hold Her hand
safe from the self-hatred below
I wait 'til kingdom come to see Her face again
In the meantime, I continue to write
with an immeasurable sense of possibility
roaring unheard underneath distant waterfalls
standing upon pink rose pedals
searching through implacable, empty skies
for just one glimpse of Her return

THE OMEGA HAS BEEN POSTPONED

Jesus has decided to hold the second Coming on another planet
to allow other life forms the opportunity
of more interesting ways of killing him
while, down on Earth,
the cult of Catholicism enjoys the materialism of crucifixes
and awaits a forced apocalypse
assuring the fanfare of his arrival by claiming everything
from New Orleans to Haiti
as proof that he loves them and only them
Despite the fact he has not even called for over two thousand years
Perhaps someday, *fua!,* he will grace us with a visit
Until then, Earth remains the asshole of the universe

COMMUNION

She wears death like yellow
alone in the desert
her blonde hair in a bun
in search of her son
once hanging from the crucifix
towering before her
All that's left behind–
the wind, a mystery,
enough wood for paper
and a note that says
'Thank you for coming'

IF JESUS WERE GAY

If Jesus were gay,
would you tattoo him to your body?
hang him from your chest?
pray to him and worship the Son of Man?
Would you still praise him after dying for your sins?

If it was revealed Jesus kissed another man,
but not on the cheek,
would you still beg him for forgiveness?
ask him for miracles?
hope your loved ones get to meet him in heaven?

If Jesus were gay,
and still loved by God and Mary
because he was their child after all
hailed by all angels and feared by demons,
would you still long to be healed by him?
take him into your home and comfort him?
heal his wounds and break bread with him?

Would wars be waged over religion?
Would world leaders invoke his name for votes?
Would churches everywhere rejoice?
and celebrate his life?
Would rappers still thank him?
in their acceptance speeches?

If the crown of thorns were placed on his head
to mock him as the "Queen of the Jews"
If he was whipped because fags are considered
sadomasochistic sodomites,
If he was crucified for the brotherhood of man
would you still repent?

Would you pray to him when you were dying?
If he didn't ask for you to be just like him,
If he only wanted you to love yourself,
If he asked that you not judge others,
Would you still wait for him to come back?
and save your soul?

Would you deny him?
Would you believe in peace?
Would there still be hate?
Would there still be hell?

Would there be laws based on the meaning
of true love?
What would Jesus do?
What would you do?

OUTSIDE

Hypocrisy exists in our world today
when those that are out can only go so far
and society is surprised when those who prefer to hide
react with violence to threats of opening closet doors
because, in darkness, they are safe from those responsible
for reducing our brothers and sisters to dust and memories
like Matthew and Brandon and Sakia and Lawrence and Jorge
and way too many others to name

Those of us that are out, in these empty rooms,
dance ignorantly to the occasional drumbeats of liberty
While the only difference between us
and those huddled in corners and shadows of fear
is that we have a little more space to breathe
Yet the smell of equality is only truly found outside
where there are no limits or debates on how to legislate desire
and sexuality is simply the right to physical expression
between consenting adults

We could live out of the closet
but we could never leave this house
Monsters,
especially those with hideous diseases and colored skin,
are not welcome in the open fields of America
where others could dare to dream
of marriage or adoption or political office
or defend our country
from imaginary weapons of mass destruction
because not all of God's children are worthy to see the light
beyond these cold white walls
We are only tolerable
as long as we remain silently lingering indoors

Straight friends sometimes visit to feed our hungry souls
with stories about journeys and adventures
Taking the time to join us and mourn the memory of our dead
before heading back into the privilege of sunlight
Leaving us behind to wave goodbye from gated windows
unable to come out and play
If only we could run past the prejudice
and feel the wind across our chests
Discover lands starving for diversity
and star filled skies waiting to shine for us too

In the distance, the emptiness of towers fallen,
a cruel reminder of our perversions and sins
as preached by religious men with tongues that are holy enough
to lick the innocence of children
to touch the openings of children
While faint sounds, unrecognizable as cries,
emerge from underneath closet doors

There are too many of us in this house
located on a land far away from Normal
Chanting songs of freedom every day
We only want to be outside,
we only want to be outside,
we only want to be outside,
The Lord is outside

It's no wonder some would rather die moths in the closet
when butterflies are not free

CLEAN

Lathering you
in the shower
after sex
Washing away
the trace
of our desire
the sins
of our world
Spilling
like secrets
Abuelas lagrimas
baptizing
this union
this purification
of soul

With these hands
a poem
I draft
across your chest
along your back
below your waist
before
you lift me up
lock lips
to drown
my tongue
with your sweet taste
the taste of me
the taste of us
together
healing
the wounds

sealing
the scars

Mi amor,
there is a war going on
outside
but beneath this rain
the only pain
is the knowledge
that there is a drought
Sooner or later
we must turn
these faucets off
return
to the reality
of people thirsting
for our blood
If only
we could stay
until the children stop dying
until mothers stop crying
until our skin wrinkles
like daddies did
like daddies did

Mi amor,
the water is warm
feels like being
inside your arms
Through the drops
in your eyes
I see a glimpse
of peace
a glimpse
of love
& I

am finally clean

A SIMPLE POEM

I want you to continue writing because I will not always be around

With lips that will never touch mine
read your poems out loud
so that the words are left engraved on the wall
make me feel your voice rush through me like a breeze from Oyá

I want to hear about Puerto Rico
about sisters with names like *La Bruja*
about educating youth about AIDS
I want to hear about life in the Boogie Down Bronx
surviving on the Down Low
don't leave out stories about men and women
you have loved and still love

I want you to write poems that you will never read
press hard on the paper so that the ink runs deep
hold the pen tight so that you control the details
prove to me that I inspire you
reveal yourself between the lines
hear my praise with each flicker of the candle
Write a poem for me

Do not choose a fresh page from a brand new journal
use paper that has been crumbled and tossed
thrown out by a spineless father only to be recycled
Save a tree for future poets to write under

Rewrite me into someone more attractive
stronger than life has made me
make me tough and sexy, aggressive like a tiger
stain the pages with cum, lube, the arousal you find
at the sight of naked boys, draw me sketches

bring the words to life with images
make me a man with this poem

Read it in front of the audience
with hidden messages just for me
be real and tell me why
I am only worth a haiku
Your epics are meant for others
I already know,
use red ink to match the blood from these wounds
with brutal honesty let me die with your last sentence

Then resurrect me with rhyme
read from your gut
let me hear the wisdom of mi *abuelo* in your voice
let me find my father in you
remind me of all the men that left me broken promises

In your eyes I want to see a poem
when you bring me to tears with painful memories
buried beneath your thick skin

Between teeth gapped like divas,
I want to hear quotes from books I never read
Make me believe you want to be a poet

Make my heart break,
tell me why you could never love me
with just a few words leave me lost and insecure
feel the admiration of others
bask in their desire
forget that I am there

Pound your fists in the air with passion
go off about politics, poverty, machismo, and hate
scream poems that don't give a fuck

about traditions, slamming or scores
save your whispers for those who make love to you

Write a poem for me that makes me want to puff a joint
A poem that loses control
unafraid to be vulnerable
for once just make me believe it is all worth letting go
when the smoke clears
I will understand
the reason I am just another face in the crowd

I want you to continue writing because I will not always be around

THE DEATH OF ART

"Reading well is one of the great pleasures that solitude can afford you" –critic Harold Bloom, who first called slam poetry "the death of art."

I am not a poet. I want to be rich and buy things for my family. Besides, I am sort of popular and can honestly say I've had a great sex life.

I am not a poet. Georgia O' Keefe paintings do absolutely nothing for me. I do not feel oppressed or depressed and no longer have anything to say about the President.

I am not a poet. I do not like being called an "activist" because it takes away from those that are out on the streets protesting and fighting for our rights.

I am not a poet. I eat poultry and fish and suck way too much dick to be considered a vegetarian.

I am not a poet. I would most likely give my ass up in prison before trying to save it with poetry . . . and I'd like it! Heck, I'd probably be inspired.

I am not a poet. I may value peace but I will not simply use a pen to unleash my anger. I would fuck somebody up if I had to.

I am not a poet. I may have been abused and had a difficult life but I don't want pity. I believe laughter and love heals.

I am not a poet. I am not dying. I write a lot about AIDS and how it has affected my life but, despite the rumors, I am not positive. Believe it or not, weight loss amongst sexually active gay men could still be a choice.

I am not a poet. I do not get Kerouac or honestly care much for Bukowski.

I am not a poet. I don't spend my weekends reading and writing. I like to go out and party. I like to have a few cocktails but I do not have a drinking problem regardless of what borough, city, or state I may wake up in.

I am not a poet. I don't need drugs to open up my imagination. I've been a dealer and had a really bad habit but that was long before I started writing.

I am not a poet. I can seriously only tolerate about half an hour of spoken word before I start tuning out and thinking about my grocery list or what my cats are up to.

I am not a poet according to the scholars and academics and Harold Bloom. I only write to masturbate my mind. After all, fucking yourself is one of the great pleasures that solitude can afford you.

I am not a poet. I am only trying to get attention and convince myself that poetry can save lives when my words simply and proudly contribute to "the death of art."

SONGS OF INNOCENCE

songs of innocence
left behind to remember
the breath ceases
childhood lasts forever
the fruition from youth to
maturity forced into truth
leaving behind broken toys
held in silence
haunting our dreams
tucked into bed at night
the desire of fathers
happiness for daughters not sorrow
goodnight, sweet princess
you have been loved
as children often are
held in arms until asleep
daddy watching over you
songs of innocence
maintain your soul alive
i read your musings
to find your smile
hear your laughter
to feel you near each day
another angel for heaven
you have more than one name
someday i hope to discover
where to find you
may the father guide us
in his knowledge in
his wisdom
goodnight, sweet princess
you have been loved

www.ingramcontent.com/pod-product-compliance
Lightning Source LLC
Chambersburg PA
CBHW051347040426
42453CB00007B/447